Building a writing career is very simple. All you need to do is write one article and get it published. After that, you write more articles and get them published. If those articles are about gardening, you have the beginning of a book on gardening…..and a writing career.

At that point, you've become an expert on gardening. You find that writing and getting articles accepted for publication seems to have become easier! You live and breathe gardening.

Editors become familiar with your work over time and soon associate your name with gardening. Then offers come to you instead of you're going after them. You're asked to speak, write articles, books and become involved in editing gardening manuscripts for accuracy and mechanical ixxues as grammar.

You've come a long way. You can live off your writing, paying bills, taking vacations and buying nice things. After all, you're a writer!

Using this book, you can avoid mistakes and save time. You will learn how to find and organize your ideas and write your first article You'll also learn how to get it published.

CHAPTER 1

To write your first article, you need something
to write about. You can write just about anything
under the sun, but for stronger and more
effective direction, you may want to draw upon
your background and career.

First, a few questions to think about and answer

 Answering questions about your chosen subject
helps to reveal aspects of it that you may have
thought about or focus on every day. But even
better, answering questions helps to uncover
stuff you can write about later on. When I taught
elementary school, for example, I read
professional journals for information on
improving my skills, providing individualized
instruction and involving students in curricular
hands-on projects. I substituted and wrote my
masster's thesis on instant reading and math
activities that substitute teachers could
implement and adapt minus a big hassle. Then in
graduate school, I included a few of those
activities in a book for teachers. My book was
published long before I graduated and copies of
it were available to professors, family and
friends. And my writing career was born.

So you see, the process took some time, but was
never boring and included money for my work. You
can also duplicate this process. earn money and
gradually create a career in writing! To begin,
it may be helpful to focus and answer a few

questions on things that are familiar to you and which you can easily discuss on your field or career. The type of training involved, for example. Where and how did you get it? What courses did you have to take and how difficult or easy were they? How long did it take to land your first position? Why would you prefer to do this job more than anything else? Would anything change and if so, what?

On the other hand, you can choose a favorite sport or hobby. Do you enjoy fantasy football? Would you rather discuss players, scores, teams and touchdowns with friends? What is your favorite NFL team and why? Have you ever bet on your team or any other team to win the Super Bowl? Do you remember the year(s) when your favorite team made the Super Bowl playoffs and later won (or lost)? Who do you consider the best (or worst) coach of all time and why?

Or maybe, you're an IT whiz and can spend a few hours consulting or working on electronic gadget issues? Do you enjoy discussing your work? Do you presently hold an IT position somewhere? How did you break in? How easy or difficult was it to get trained? How much is the pay? What perks are available? Do you train others? What aspects do you dislike or even hate?

When you think about these things, you may realize that there are any number of aspects to write about in an article.

Right now, however, we'll focus on finding and using a good article topic and after doing that, locating and "preselling" a few markets.

At this point, you've decided on a topic for your article. That was the first step. The next step is assigning a working title and deciding what kind of article to write.

CHAPTER 2

In this chapter, you'll learn how to create the type of article that you'd like to write and presell it to the right market before you actually write it.

You heard correctly. It's a win-win situation for you and the potential editor. You save time and effort by finding out in advance if you have a viable idea. The editor also saves time by reading your query letter and deciding whether your proposed article Is right for his or her magazine.

Magazines need writers, especially writers who contact them with good article ideas and articles that readers want to read.

Ok, so we'll begin with your topic. Let's say that you've chosen tennis and want to write an article on tennis. Right away, you've got a problem because there's no way that your article will (or should) include everything there is to know about tennis. But if you focus in on the positions that tennis champions use to handle and maneuver a tennis racket or secrets of their endurance, you just might have an article idea that will tempt an editor! See, you've focused on one or rwo aspects of the game instead of tennis in a general sense and taken advantage of the fact that many tennis players would love to know and practice those secrets, improving their game and maybe reaching the "pro" status at some

point. And those players will be mighty
interested in reading the article in that tennis
magazine. Now the editor is also interested and
continues reading, wondering what the article
will include. Maybe it will mention three or four
winning strategies for manipulating the racket or
building up endurance and strength. Or maybe
your article will include an interview with a
tennis champion!

Content like that is very persuasive and
convincing an editor to assign that article to
you. Since the editor doesn't know you or how
well you can write or meet deadlines, he or she
will likely let you work on the assignment on
speculation, meaning that if your finished
article meets his or her expectations, you'll be
paid and see your words in print! You love tennis
and will likely write more articles on some
aspects of it, maybe a lot of articles that you
can organize into chapters for a book! All of
that will happen in time. Just keep writing and
don't ever give up, especially after your first
article is published. That first published
article will form part of the foundation in
building up your writing career, so you need to
hang in and give it your best shot.

CHAPTER 3

Now that you've got a topic and are ready to
focus on one or two aspects of it, you should

Develop a working title. Using our tennis article
example, you may be able to create "How to
Improve Your Swing" or "Three Ways to Outlast
Your Opponent." When writing your query letter,

mention this working title and briefly describe
two or

three key highlights in order to tempt the
editor. That description will appear in your
letter's second paragraph. And your third or
final paragraph should describe your own tennis-
related background. Maybe you played and excelled
in tennis in college. Maybe you taught the game
at summer camp or the Y. Or maybe you took
courses in tennis to satisfy degree or
certification requirements for a degree in
physical education. **Mentioning related background**

is convincing, letting an editor know that you
have some expertise in tennis and are just the
writer she's looking for!

Finding a suitable markets for your article

Looking in the Writer's Market is the next step.
Turn to the magazine publishers section and look
for sports magazines. You may find a few
magazines on tennis. Jot down the editor's name
(or assistant editor's name), address, phone
number, e-mail address. Find out if that magazine
accepts e-mailed query letters.

Back home, draft final copies of your query
letters and submit them to each editor. Be
prepared to wait a few weeks or months or weeks

for a reply. In the meantime, brainstorm more
tennis article ideas and begin writing query
letters to editors in appropriate magazines.
Remember to note down the dates of submission in
a notebook or in a folder in your computer.

F

CHAPTER 4

Let's say that an editor replied, stating that he
or she will be happy to see your article on
speculation. Again, submitting an article on spec
means that there's no guarantee that it will be
accepted for publication. The only guarantee is
that your article will receive careful
consideration. Even if it is well written and
organized, but if a similar article is being
considered by a known author, your article could
be rejected. Still, an editor may have liked it

and encourages you to submit more article ideas. He or she will usually write a note on the

rejection slip. If that happens to you, by all means, submit your ideas in the next few days. You will stand a better chance of having your work accepted for publication and receiving more article assignments as well!

In addition, an editor may like your work so much that he or she may ask you to work as a "contributing editor." A contributing editor is a freelance writer who receives article assignments from the magazine. As a contributing editor, your name would appear in the magazine's masthead. You would be expected to discuss possible ideas with editors and receive definite article assignments. Having served a few years ago as Instructor magazine's contributing editor, I should know. It was great in terms of assignments and pay. I enjoyed researching and having assignments come to me rather than having to earn assignments all of the time. It became another building block in my early writing career, a credit that I could mention in my resume and in a brief description as an author of a published book.

CHAPTER 5

Having a single article published, you have
leverage in building up your writing career. By
all means, mention that credit in future query
letters and resumes. Remember to include it in
your book proposal, make copies of it to use as
writing samples for publishers that you contact.
After all, you're a published writer now!

Write a book!

Rather than waiting too long, start writing a
book on your subject. As you did in early work on
your first article, you should create a working
title and an outline. In this case, a list of
chapters with titles may be a good way to begin a
book. Your book will, for example, focus on how
to get started playing tennis, equipment, rules
and clothing. Or maybe your book will be devoted

To a tennis champion known for his or her
endurance and winning attitude. A likely book can
focus on the most effective ways to play and
where and how to buy the best equipment, what to
look for and how to avoid wasting time and money.
Once you're sure about your book's focus, create
a working title, table of contents, and 2 to 5
sample chapters. Long ago, editors were satisfied
in a single sample chapter, but with rising costs
and oompetition among publishers and writers,
submitting multiple sample chapters as part of a
book proposal is the new norm nowadays.

On the other hand, you may just want to avoid
that traditional route and self-publish your book
instead. Remember, though, that you'll be
responsible for artwork, editing, binding, book
cover formatting, and promotion. A good
alternative option is working on a similar
existing project for a book producer. However,
the author of that book, and not you, will
receive credit.

When it comes down to wriing a book, did you know
that each chapter is really an article? You can
write a single article in a day, or week. Knowing
how long it takes you to write an article makes
it easier to estimate how long it will take you
to write a nonfiction book. So if you write an
article/chapter in one week, then you'll need ten
weeks' time to complete a book containing ten
chapters. If you can write two articles per week,
your book will be done in roughly five weeks, or

in little more than a month. In addition to time for writing, you'll need to budget some time for proofreadind and editing. Maybe one or two items in your chapters need facts or a little more explanation or clarification. Maybe statistics need to be included or explained. Maybe certain points need to be clarified. Subtle things like these are very subtle and don't tend to be obvious as long as you are still developing content. That's because you're still too close to your writing to pick that up while your work is still hot off the press.

In checking your work, pay attention to margin size and paragraph length. As a rule, no page should ever contain a single paragraph that is a page in length. It's much too long for readers to cope with. It's also a turn-off. Readers may simply opt to skip that page altogether rather than bothering to read a lengthy paragraph. So make things easier by cutting paragraph size if its length is excessively long.

Taking care of details like proofing and editing now will save time and needless aggravation later.

CHAPTER 7

Beginning to write your book

Points to remember

. Planning and writing a book takes time and effort.

. Material, such as articles, can be organiaed into your book, but may need to be re-edited and rewritten.

You should work on your book for about an hour every day at a time most convenint for you, such as mornings, aftenoons or evenings.

. Begin your book by jotting down a list of chapter titles and developing a working title.

. Review your work the next day and make necessary additions, corrections, deletions as necessary. Or switch the sequence of chapter sub-tles.

. put your work away if you feel too tired or ill. /ait until you are feeling better.

. Write a draft of your book's first three chapters and do the best job possible. These chapters will beoome part of your proposal at some future point. You can count on ediors re-questing sample chapters.

. Budget enough time for writing, proofing and ediing your book.

Be ready to jot down ideas as they occur to you
for articles and your book's chapters.

. Start perusing Writer' Market for possible book
publishers. Make a note of publishers who would
be interested in your book and their submission
guidelines. Also, consider getting an agent.

. In the meantime, explore opportunities for
talks that you can give at aassociations,
libraries, and civic organizations. Select a
problem that you will discuss in your speech that
is related to your book's subject.

. Use your book's chapter titles as ideas for
more articles, talks, books and e-books. Become
acquainted with bookstore owners and managers.

CHAPTER 8

As you probably have come to realize, there is no
single path moving you from writing and
publishing articles to writing books. Much will
depends on your motivation, talent, and efforts
to promote your work and yourself. You will
realize more money and opportunities and notice
that you receive offers to consult, read, and
speak as time goes on.

I wish you every success and invite you to let me
know about articles and books you've written and
have published as a result. Use the line,
published book/article in your subject line and
email me at DAZZ415@aol.com

t

x